D1611864

TECHNOLOGIES
AND
STRATEGIES
IN BATTLE

THE BATTLE OF
MARATHON

Earle Rice Jr.

Mitchell Lane
PUBLISHERS

P.O. Box 196
Hockessin, Delaware 19707
Visit us on the web: www.mitchelllane.com
Comments? email us: mitchelllane@mitchelllane.com

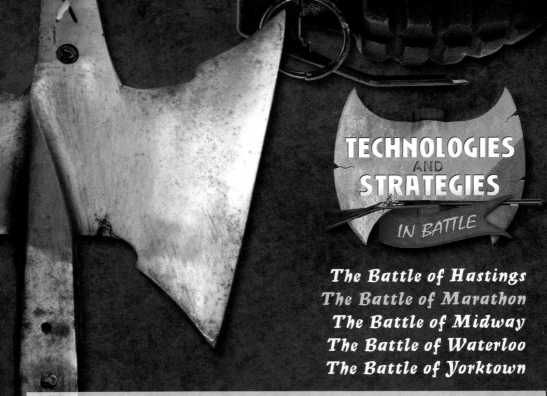

TECHNOLOGIES AND STRATEGIES

IN BATTLE

The Battle of Hastings
The Battle of Marathon
The Battle of Midway
The Battle of Waterloo
The Battle of Yorktown

PUBLISHER'S NOTE: The facts on which the story
in this book is based have been thoroughly
researched. Documentation of such research
can be found on page 45. While every possible
effort has been made to ensure accuracy, the
publisher will not assume liability for damages
caused by inaccuracies in the data, and
makes no warranty on the accuracy of the
information contained herein.

ABOUT THE AUTHOR: Earle Rice Jr. is a former
senior design engineer and technical writer in
the aerospace, electronic defense, and
nuclear industries. He has devoted full time to
his writing since 1993 and is the author of more
than sixty published books. Earle is listed in
Who's Who in America and is a member of the
Society of Children's Book Writers and
Illustrators, the League of World War I Aviation
Historians, the Air Force Association, and the
Disabled American Veterans.

To reflect current usage, we have chosen to
use the secular era designations BCE ("before
the common era") and CE ("of the common
era") instead of the traditional designations BC
("before Christ") and AD (*anno Domini*, "in the
year of the Lord").

Printing   1   2   3   4   5   6   7   8   9

**Library of Congress
Cataloging-in-Publication Data**

Rice, Earle.
 The Battle of Marathon / by Earle Rice, Jr.
    p. cm. — (Technologies and strategies in
battle)
 Includes bibliographical references and index.
 ISBN 978-1-61228-077-6 (library bound)
 1. Marathon, Battle of, Greece, 490 B.C.—
Juvenile literature. I. Title.
 DF225.4.R53 2011
 938'.03—dc22
                                            2011000606

eBook ISBN: 9781612281599
                                                       PLB

CONTENTS

Greek mythology lauds Achilles (ah-KIL-eez) as the bravest and strongest Greek warrior in the Trojan War. Over time, mythology slowly gave way to recorded history. Living, breathing, real-life heroes began to replace storybook icons of great courage and daring. One such warrior was Miltiades (mil-TEE-uh-deez) of Athens. He reportedly descended from the grandfather of Achilles. Thus, the blood of Achilles flowed in the veins of Miltiades—the future hero of the Battle of Marathon. This is the story of that battle, and of how Miltiades used the weapons and strategies of his time to seize victory in the face of near-certain defeat.

More than a half millennium before the Common Era, the Persian Empire covered most of the then known world. In 512 BCE, Darius I of Persia (now Iran) began to feel threatened by Greece's far-reaching trade routes. Its water routes stretched from the shores of eastern Spain to the far end of the Black Sea. Darius felt that Western traders were encroaching on the land and sea routes of Persia's own eastern traders. Bitter rivalries between East and West soon developed. War inevitably followed.

The Vengeance of Darius

Darius ordered his armies across the Bosporus (BOS-por-us), the narrow strait separating Turkey in Europe and Asia. His invincible armies invaded Scythia (SIH-thee-uh), an ancient section of Europe and Asia that now makes up parts of Ukraine, Russia, and Kazakhstan (kah-zok-STON). As they continued westward, the unstoppable Persian legions added Thrace and Macedonia in the Balkan Peninsula to their conquests. By the time Darius retired to his eastern capitals, he had greatly expanded his realm. It then stretched from India to the Mediterranean Sea. The world had never before known the likes of the vast and powerful Persian Empire.

By 510, only one important nation—Greece—remained outside the grasp of Darius and his undefeated armies. But in seeking to stem the development

and expansion of Greece, and to add his western neighbor to his conquests, Darius awakened his future conqueror. He had hardly heard of the tiny city-state that would later topple his empire. "The Athenians," he asked at the time, "who are they?"[1] He would find out all too soon.

Between 510 and 506, the Athenians overthrew their tyrannical ruler Hippias and drove him out of their city-state. An aristocrat named Cleisthenes (KLEES-thuh-neez) led the Athenian revolt. He and his followers reestablished order in the city-state and much more. They imposed reforms that changed the basis of organization from family and clan to locality. Further, they replaced the existing four blood clans with ten local tribes. Each tribe had representation from city, coast, and hill areas.

As part of his reforms, Cleisthenes created a group of citizens called the Council of Five Hundred. Its members were chosen each year by lot to draft new laws and policies. The existing Citizens Assembly, with expanded powers, debated and voted on the Council's recommendations. In annual free elections, citizens chose three archons (AR-kons) to preside over the government, and ten military generals—the *strategoi*—to command the army. Cleisthenes based his reforms on a credo of "equal rights for all." At the close of the sixth century BCE, Athens prepared to enter a new century as the world's first true democratic body.

In the meantime, the deposed tyrant Hippias remained resentful over the loss of both pride and position. He blamed the "democrats" of Athens for destroying his former state. With traitorous intentions, he fled to Sardis (now part of Turkey). He planned to seek help from the Persian satrap (SAY-trap; governor) in restoring his power. In return, Hippias offered to hold Attica (eastern Greece) under Persian rule. His pleas failed when the Persian-ruled Greek cities of Asia Minor suddenly banished their satraps and declared their independence. Hippias sought further refuge in the court of Darius. He would later play an important role at Marathon.

While these events were unfolding, another key player at Marathon was building a reputation as a warrior to be reckoned

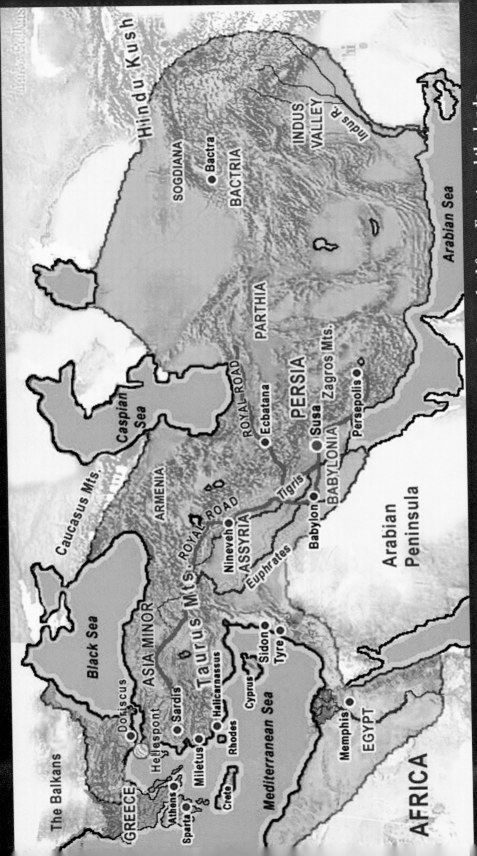

By the end of the reign of Darius I, the Persian Empire (in orange) stretched from Egypt and the lands east of Greece to beyond the Indus Valley in present-day Pakistan and western India.

with. Miltiades the Younger—named after his uncle, Miltiades the Elder—was also demonstrating a keen ability to look after his own best interests. Around 516 BCE, Miltiades the Younger (hereinafter simply Miltiades) traveled to the Thracian Chersonese (now the Gallipoli Peninsula) to settle the affairs of his dead brother, Stesagoras (steh-SAA-guh-rus).

Upon his arrival in the Chersonese, Miltiades set about to establish himself as its new ruler. Pretending to mourn his brother's death, he stayed shut up at home. Local leaders soon arrived to offer their condolences for the death of his sibling. "Miltiades commanded them to be seized and thrown into prison,"[2] wrote Greek historian Herodotus (huh-RAH-duh-tus). To secure his position, he formed a bodyguard of 500 mercenaries and then married Hegesipyle (hey-guh-SIH-pih-lee). She was the daughter of the Thracian king Olorus. Hegesipyle would later bear her husband a son named Cimon.

In 513 BCE, Miltiades fell under the sway of the advancing Persians. He was forced to join Darius in an expedition against the Scythians. When Darius suffered reverses in the Scythian wilderness, he left Miltiades and his fellow Greeks in charge of the bridge over the Danube. On learning of Darius's troubles, Miltiades suggested to his companions that they strand Darius by destroying the bridge. "The rulers of the Asiatic Greek cities, whom Miltiades addressed," wrote historian Edward Shepherd Creasy, "shrank from this bold but ruthless stroke against the Persian power, and Darius returned in safety."[3] Miltiades fled.

Darius soon learned of Miltiades's deceit. Creasy continued: "[T]he vengeance of Darius was thenceforth specially directed against the man who had counseled such a deadly blow against his empire and his person."[4] His burning desire for vengeance would smolder for more than two decades and finally set the ancient world aflame at Marathon.

**Helmet given by Miltiades as a sacrifice
at the Temple of Zeus in Olympia**

Darius the Great

Darius I was the son of the satrap (governor) of Parthia, a province of the Persian Empire now in Iran. Known as Darius the Great, he rose to power in the manner of a tyrant. (In his time, a tyrant was anyone—either good or bad—who established his rule by force.) He ascended the throne of Persia in 522 BCE by killing a pretender to the throne named Gaumata. "Gathering half a dozen chiefs about him," wrote historian Alan Lloyd, "Darius burst into the castle where Gaumata was staying and slew him before he had time to call his guards out."[5] In so doing, Darius restored the throne to the Achaemenian (ak-uh-MEE-nee-un) dynasty.

He met immediate resistance to his ascendance by assassination. By 519, however, Darius and his generals managed to establish his authority in the east by defeating nine rebel leaders in nineteen battles. After restoring internal order in his new empire, he embarked on a series of campaigns to strengthen his frontiers and secure them against nomadic incursions. That same year, Darius attacked the Scythians east of the Caspian Sea. A few years later, he conquered the Indus Valley.

In 513, having subdued eastern Thrace, Darius crossed the Danube River into European Scythia. The retreating Scythians devastated the land as they fled before the Persians. Darius overextended his supply lines and was forced to abandon his campaign. Satraps of Asia Minor then took a hand in finishing the subjugation of Thrace, subduing Macedonia, and seizing the Aegean Islands of Lemnos and Imbros. By the turn of a new century, Darius and the Persians stood on the threshold of Greece and the Western world.

Fifth-century BCE
akinakes, **worn from a belt on the right side of the body**

Chapter 2

The Persian Empire actually reached the Aegean Sea during the reign of Cyrus II in 547 BCE. Known as Cyrus the Great, he was the founder of the Achaemenian dynasty. He came to power by overthrowing his maternal grandfather, Astyages (as-TY-ah-geez), the king of Media. (The ancient country of Media occupied the plateau region just south of the Caspian Sea in present-day Iran. The Medes were closely related to the Persians in custom and culture.) Under Cyrus II and his son Cambyses II, the empire's westward expansion largely stopped at the Aegean Sea. Persian advances were focused elsewhere until Darius I took the throne. A rekindled Persian interest in the west began with his unsuccessful campaign against Scythia in 513 BCE.

After withdrawing from Scythia, Darius spent the next year in Sardis. A year later, he returned to his winter residence in Susa. (The ruins of the ancient city of Susa can still be seen at the village of Shush in southwest Iran). Darius left his brother, Artaphernes (ar-tuh-FUR-nez) the Elder, as satrap in Sardis. Meanwhile, his generals, first Megabazos and then Otanes, continued to bring

The Ionian Revolt

Europe south of Scythia slowly under Persian control. During this time, unrest began to stir in Ionia, a coastal region of Asia Minor bordering the Aegean Sea.

Ionia was never a political entity; rather, it was essentially a religious league made up of ten mainland city-states and two island city-states. It had been subjugated by Persia for almost a half century. In 500 BCE, the Ionians suddenly and almost at the same time sent away or killed their Persian satraps. Aristagoras (ar-ih-STAG-uh-rus), the governor of Miletus (mih-LEE-tus), secretly organized the beginnings of a revolt against Persian rule. Miletus, on the coast of Caria in Asia Minor, was the southernmost and most important of the Twelve Ionian Cities. It took the lead in what came to be known as the Ionian Revolt.

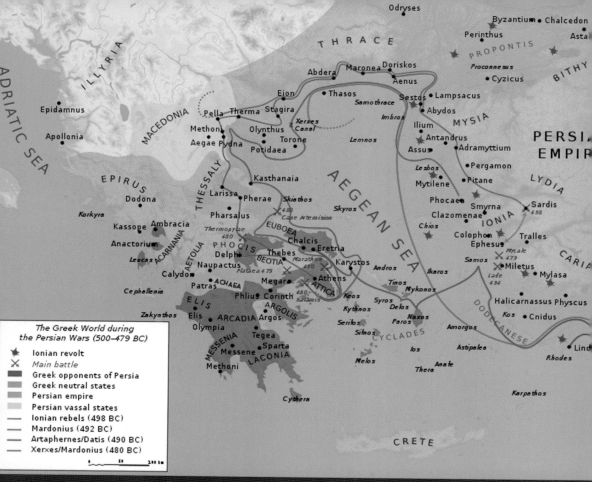

The Greek World during
the Persian Wars (500–479 BC)

★ Ionian revolt
✕ Main battle
▬ Greek opponents of Persia
▬ Greek neutral states
▬ Persian empire
▬ Persian vassal states
— Ionian rebels (498 BC)
— Mardonius (492 BC)
— Artaphernes/Datis (490 BC)
— Xerxes/Mardonius (480 BC)

The Battle of Marathon, fought in 490 BCE, was a turning point in the Persian Wars against Greece. Xerxes I, the son and successor of Darius I, invaded Greece in 480 BCE to avenge the defeat of his father's army at Marathon. The Persians broke through the pass at Thermopylae and pillaged Athens, but then lost their fleet in the Battle of Salamis. After Greek hoplites slaughtered Persian forces at Plataea in 479 BCE, Xerxes withdrew from Greece. His withdrawal marked the beginning of the decline of the Persian Empire.

Aristagoras recognized that he would need outside help in confronting the mighty Persians. He sought aid from King Cleomenes (klee-OH-muh-neez) I of Sparta without success. The king did not want to become involved in what promised to be mostly a naval action. Aristagoras, as Will Durant put it, "passed on to Athens, mother city of many Ionian towns, and

pleaded so well that the Athenians sent a fleet of twenty ships to support the revolt."[1] The Eretrians helped out with another five triremes, ancient galleys with three banks of oars. Eretria (eh-REE-tree-uh) was a city founded as an Ionian colony on Euboea (yew-BEE-uh), an island north of Attica in the Aegean Sea. The combined fleet landed in Ephesus (EF-uh-sus), one of the Twelve Ionian Cities, in 499.

A typical trireme measured about 120 feet (37 meters) in overall length, with a beam (width) of 18 feet (5.5 meters). It achieved its propulsive power from 170 oarsmen arranged in three tiers along each side of the vessel. Fourteen *thranites* (THRA-nyts), rowers in the upper bank, pulled on 14-foot oars; 27 *zygites* (ZY-gyts), rowers in the middle bank, on 10-foot, 6-inch oars; and 27 *thalamites* (THAL-uh-mites), rowers in the lower bank, on 7-foot, 6-inch oars.

Depending on the strength and stamina of its rowers, a trireme could reach a speed greater than 7 knots (8 miles per hour, or 13 kilometers per hour), but only for a short period. The trireme also bore sails for running before favorable winds. Sails were lowered and stowed along its centerline when entering battle.

The trireme, an oar-powered warship, was light, fast, and maneuverable. It was the principal naval vessel used by Persia and the Greek city-states as they vied for mastery of the Mediterranean during the Greco-Persian Wars.

Triremes were armed with a long, bronze-tipped ram at its prow for piercing and sinking enemy vessels. They also carried a few archers and soldiers for boarding opposing galleys.

"Meanwhile," Durant continued, "the Ionians were acting with a chaotic vigor characteristic of the Greeks; each rebel city raised its own troops, but kept them under separate command; and the Milesian army, led with more bravery than wisdom, marched upon Sardis and burned the great city to the ground."[2]

The razing of Sardis—the principal Persian city in Asia Minor—took place in 498. Herodotus, the leading source of original material about Greek history, gave this account of the raid:

> [T]he houses in Sardis were most of them built of reeds . . . one of them was no sooner fired by a soldier than the flames ran speedily from house to house, and spread over the whole place. As the fire raged, the Lydians and such Persians as were in the city, inclosed on every side by the flames . . . and finding themselves unable to get out, came in crowds to the market-place . . . [and] were forced to stand on their defence.[3]

The marauding Greeks had not come prepared for a prolonged encounter with the Persians. When battle-hardened Persian soldiers from nearby garrisons rushed to the aid of their besieged countrymen in Sardis, the raiders fled toward the Aegean coast. The Persians pursued them with all due speed. "The Ionians drew out against them in battle array;" noted Herodotus, "and a fight ensued, wherein the Greeks had very greatly the worse. Vast numbers were slain by the Persians."[4] Those who escaped the wrath of their pursuers—including Miltiades of Athens—scattered back to their several city-states.

The burning of Sardis enraged Darius I. His enmity particularly extended to the Athenians and the Eretrians for their participation in the revolt of the Ionians. According to Herodotus, he shot an arrow into the sky and said, "Grant me, Jupiter, to revenge

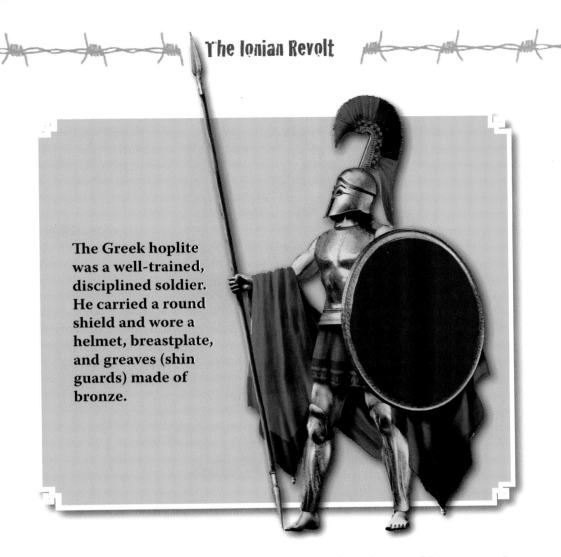

The Greek hoplite was a well-trained, disciplined soldier. He carried a round shield and wore a helmet, breastplate, and greaves (shin guards) made of bronze.

myself on the Athenians!"[5] Further, he ordered one of his servants to repeat to him three times each day at dinner these words: "Master, remember the Athenians."[6] For the rest of his life, Darius would never forget—or forgive—the Athenians.

Over the next four years, Darius gradually bracketed the Ionian forces between his land armies and the sea. By then, a huge Persian fleet of 600 warships controlled the eastern Aegean. Under Artaphernes, the Persian fleet began a blockade of Miletus. A lesser but gallant Ionian fleet of 353 ships made a last-ditch effort to break the blockade and defeat the Persian armada. The two fleets clashed near the tiny island of Lade, not far from Miletus.

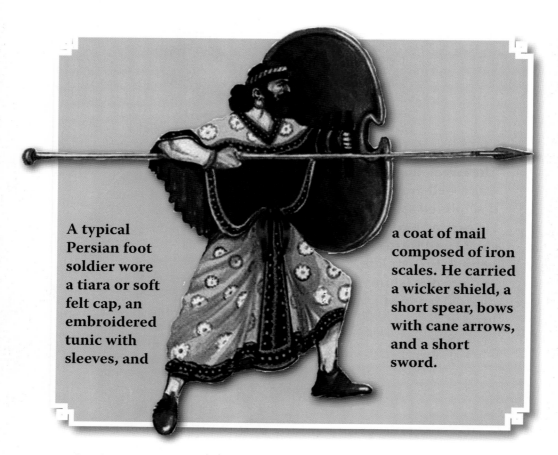

A typical Persian foot soldier wore a tiara or soft felt cap, an embroidered tunic with sleeves, and a coat of mail composed of iron scales. He carried a wicker shield, a short spear, bows with cane arrows, and a short sword.

At the start of the fighting, about a third of the already vastly outnumbered Ionian fleet fled the battle. A naval contingent from the island of Samos had secretly come to terms with the Persian satrap. Its flight from the sea encounter prompted other contingents to follow. Artaphernes and his fleet won the great sea battle virtually by default. In the aftermath of the sea fighting, the Persians seized Miletus and reduced it to a minor town from that day forward. Darius reinstated Persian rule throughout Ionia, and the Ionian Revolt ended in 494 BCE.

Darius next turned his eyes toward Greece. "Little Athens," observed Will Durant, "as the result of her generous assistance to her daughter cities, found herself face to face with an empire literally a hundred times greater than Attica."[7]

The Persians

Cyrus II—Cyrus the Great of Persia—won a great empire in the sixth century BCE. He began his reign as the ruler of the Medes, a people similar to the Persians. His empire centered on Persia and included Media, Ionia, Lydia, Mesopotamia, Syria, and Palestine. In his time, warfare departed from simple butchery between armed barbarians and took the first steps toward becoming modernized. This era saw the beginnings of training for troops, the introduction of tactics, and the use of refined weapons. Under Cyrus II, the Persian army became the first great army of its age.

The Persians used all the weapons available to them—bows, spears, swords, and axes. They also used every available delivery system—horse cavalry, both light and heavy infantry, and even chariots (though their usefulness was already declining). Light infantry basically consisted of archers who sometimes carried daggers and axes. Heavy infantry carried shields, short spears, axes, and other weapons. Among all their weapons, the bow ranked supreme. Persian archers, both mounted and unmounted, delivered storms of arrows with deadly efficiency.

Persian tactics favored engaging the enemy at a distance. Horse-archers and light-infantry bowmen fired in successive waves. After the archers had created confusion and gaps in the enemy formations, the Persians would close to finish him. According to Herodotus, the Persian army had 29 corps of 60,000 men each.[8] Its ranks included soldiers from various conquered countries. This diverse makeup introduced an inherent weakness caused by differences of arms, equipment, and training.

Persian chariot relief

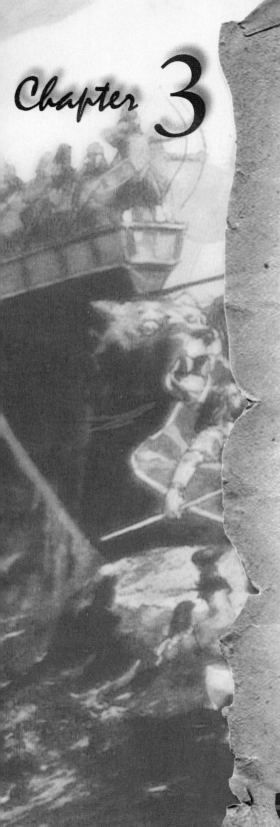

In 492 BCE, Darius I decided the time was right to avenge the burning of Sardis. As a first step in dealing with the Greeks, he sent an army into Thrace to prepare a base for mainland operations. He named Mardonius, who was both his nephew and his son-in-law, to command the army and lead the operation. Mardonius's first priority was to reconquer Thrace and punish it for its role in the Ionian Revolt. This he did in only a few months. He had then planned to march south along the mainland coast to attack Eretria and Athens. His fleet was to follow along by sea. An unexpected storm upset his plan, however. Along the way, wrote Herodotus,

A violent north wind sprang up, against which nothing could contend, and handled a large number of ships with much rudeness, shattering them and driving them aground. . . . [T]he number of ships destroyed was little short of three hundred; and the men who perished were more than twenty thousand.[1]

Drama at Marathon

Adding to Mardonius's troubles, a Thracian tribe struck his land forces in a surprise night attack, slaying great numbers of Persians. Faced with such crippling losses, he returned to Asia Minor with the remnants of his mainland expedition. Mardonius had subdued Thrace and Macedonia, but he had failed to establish a mainland base for the invasion of Greece. Fate had spared Eretria and Athens from imminent attack, but not for long.

Darius became more determined than ever to triumph over Athens, perhaps, as some scholars believe, as a prelude to conquering all of Greece. He immediately ordered a fleet to be built and an army assembled. He planned an amphibious assault on the Athenians. This time, he would send his invaders

Greek war helmet

directly across the Aegean Sea. To command the amphibious force, he named Datis, a Median general, and Artaphernes the Younger, his nephew. (Though Darius named two commanders, most scholars recognize Datis as the overall commander.) According to Herodotus, Darius ordered them "to carry Athens and Eretria away captive, and to bring the prisoners into his presence."[2]

While his forces were assembling in 491 BCE, Darius sent envoys to the various city-states in Greece to demand samples of "earth and water." Accepting such demands was a traditional sign of submission. Most of the islands and some of the smaller mainland city-states were intimidated by the Persian demands and complied. The Athenians said they would never submit and sent the envoys away. The Spartans used less diplomacy: They tossed the messengers down a deep well, telling them that they would find plenty of earth and water at the bottom. Their defiant act did little to quench Darius's thirst of revenge.

In July of 490 BCE, Datis and Artaphernes the Younger left the court of Darius and assembled their invasion forces at Cilicia, an ancient coastal city in southeast Asia Minor. After loading troops and horses, "the whole fleet, amounting to six hundred triremes," wrote Herodotus, "made sail for Ionia."[3] Herodotus omitted any mention of troop figures. The best modern estimates of Persian troop strength range between 20,000 and 50,000 men. Hippias, the long-deposed Athenian tyrant, sailed among them to serve as a guide and adviser.

From the Ionian isle of Samos, the fleet turned westward and crossed the Aegean Sea to the Cyclades (SIK-luh-deez), a group of about 220 islands. Threading their way northward through the island group, the fleet "landed here and there," notes military historian Terrence Poulos, "settling old scores and trying to pick up more recruits."[4] These skirmishes occurred in early August and are known as the Cyclades Campaign. In late August, the fleet sailed on to Euboea. Datis landed part of his forces and laid siege to the city of Eretria.

Meanwhile, about thirty miles to the south, the Athenians were engaged in the Panathenaic (pan-ath-uh-NAY-ik) Games. These games were held every four years in Athens. Hosted in a stadium, they incorporated religious festivals, athletic competitions, and cultural events. Callimachus (kuh-LIM-uh-kuhs) of Aphidna entered those games of August 490 BCE and came away a celebrated victor. He would soon compete at a much higher level in a far deadlier game.

Miltiades, the ex-soldier and former tyrant of the Chersonese, was also present in Athens that August. When the Persians reached the island of Tenedos (now Bozcaada) during the Ionian Revolt, he had escaped to Athens. After his return, he had survived a trial for tyranny and reentered Athenian political life. Miltiades was well-traveled and in his early sixties by then. But in the theater of human conflict, he had yet to take the stage for the performance of his life. And the curtain was about to go up.

Back in Eretria, the Persian attack lasted for eight days. On the seventh day, the Persians entered the city. As reported by Herodotus, they "no sooner entered within the walls than they plundered and burnt all the temples that were in the town, in revenge for the burning of their own temples at Sardis."[5] Several days later, Datis sailed for Attica.

Persian helmet

Hippias guided the Persians to Marathon, explaining that its plain was the most suitable site for cavalry action and the closest to Eretria. He also directed the off-loading of Persian forces and set

The Persians anchored in the Bay of Marathon and encamped at Schinias Beach. A present-day reconstruction of the campsite depicts several beached Persian vessels prior to the historic battle at Marathon.

up their order of battle at Marathon. Datis agreed to the landing site based on assurances from Hippias that the region would rise up in support of them, as it had for his father more than a half-century earlier. They would soon learn, however, that times and loyalties had changed under the new Athenian democracy.

"When intelligence of this [the Persian landing] reached the Athenians," wrote Herodotus, "they likewise marched their troops to Marathon, and there stood on the defensive, having at their head ten generals, of whom one was Miltiades."[6] And it was he who stood forth to play the lead role in the impending drama at Marathon.

Plain of Marathon

Modern view of the Plain of Marathon

At the beginning of September 490 BCE, Hippias guided Datis, Artaphernes, and their Persian army to the Bay of Marathon. The great Persian fleet crossed the narrow channel separating the island of Euboea from Attica and drew up at Schinias Beach at the east end of the bay. Thousands of Persian troops flowed ashore onto a broad level field ideally suited for battle. This was the Plain of Marathon.

Named for the wild fennel (*marathos*) that still grows there, the Plain of Marathon measures 5 miles (8 kilometers) long and 2 miles (3 kilometers) wide and borders on the bay. At the east end of the plain, Lake Stomi provided a water source for Persian troops and horses. The Great Marsh, north of the beach, restricted the use of cavalry in that area.

The broad open plain roughly centers on the half-moon-shaped bay. Standing within a sacred grove in the southwest corner of the plain, the Sanctuary of Heracles (Hercules) served as a campsite for the Athenian army. The grove and surrounding trees offered some protection to the Athenians. To the south and east, the Vrexiza marsh and the ancient town of Marathon bordered the grove and the bay. Farther to the west, across the road to Athens, the slopes of Mount Agrieliki offer a commanding view of the battlefield.

On the Plain of Marathon, 10,000 Athenians and 1,000 Plataeans (pluh-TEE-uns) faced at least double their numbers of Persians in defense of the first democracy.

Chapter 4

News of the Persian landing at Marathon found the *strategoi*—the ten military leaders of Athens—still in the city. Their first action was to send the runner Pheidippides (fy-DIH-puh-deez) to Sparta with a request for aid. The Spartans said they would be happy to help, but they could not leave Sparta until the moon was full (in about two weeks) because of a religious festival in progress. Unable to wait that long, the Athenian commanders decided to march their army to Marathon right away.

The Athenians proceeded to Marathon, where they set up camp in the Grove of Heracles. Their army numbered about 10,000 hoplites, heavily armed and armored infantry soldiers. The Athenians had gathered an army after receiving a call for help from the Eretrians. Each of the ten Athenian tribes sent 1,000 men with an elected general. A volunteer group of 1,000 additional hoplites from Plataea (pluh-TEE-uh) joined them at Marathon. (Plataea was a city-state long allied with Athens.) Overall command of the Greeks was shared by Miltiades, one of the ten elected generals, and Callimachus, the polemarch, a selected official

Saving
Athens

who led the army on the march and anchored its right wing.

"When the Greeks arrived at Marathon, they deployed above the plain and between two rivers," writes Terrence Poulos. "The Greeks thereby blocked the route off the beach to Athens," which was between 24 and 26 miles away.[1] A stalemate persisted for the next eight days. The Greeks felt reluctant to leave their defensive position, while the Persians appeared unwilling or unready to attack it.

At some point—either before leaving Athens or after arriving at Marathon—the Greek leaders gathered for a war council. Five of the generals felt that their forces were too small to attack the much larger Persian forces. They opted not to fight. The other five generals, championed by Miltiades, voted to fight at

once. Miltiades, as noted by Herodotus, called on Callimachus to cast the deciding vote:

> On thee therefore we depend in this matter, which lies wholly in thine own power. Thou hast only to add thy vote to my side and thy country will be free, and not free only, but the first state in Greece. Or, if thou preferrest to give thy vote to them who would decline the combat, then the reverse will follow.[2]

Callimachus likely figured what life would be like if they yielded to Persian demands to surrender. It would mean giving everything to the Persians and the return of Hippias as tyrant. Callimachus voted to fight.

Under the Athenian military system, each elected general took a daily turn at command. Miltiades waited until the day of his turn—probably September 21—then deployed his forces on the plain. With the Persian cavalry apparently watering its horses across the fast-flowing Charadra to the north, Miltiades hoped to force a quick, decisive action to the south. The Greeks fanned out across the plain for almost a mile, with the Athenians on the right wing and the Plataeans to their left. Similarly, the Persians arrayed to face them. Estimates of Persian numbers vary widely—anywhere from 12,000 to about four times the strength of the Greek forces.

"Now, as they marshalled the host upon the field of Marathon," wrote Herodotus, "in order that the Athenian front might be of equal length with the Median [Persian], the ranks of the centre were diminished, and it became the weakest part of the line, while the wings were both made strong with a depth of many ranks."[3]

The Greeks used the phalanx as their standard military formation. It was made up of spearmen formed in a unit usually eight ranks deep. At Marathon, to match up against the larger

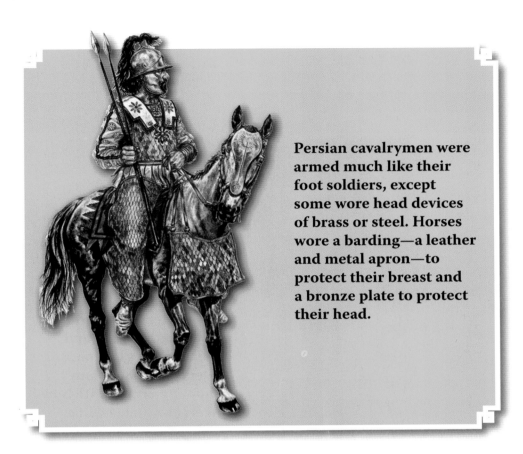

Persian cavalrymen were armed much like their foot soldiers, except some wore head devices of brass or steel. Horses wore a barding—a leather and metal apron—to protect their breast and a bronze plate to protect their head.

Persian force, Miltiades was forced to reduce his center to four ranks deep. His flanks remained at eight—or, as some say, possibly increased to twelve—ranks deep.

Because Greek forces consisted only of hoplite infantrymen armed with spears and short swords, Miltiades depended on the speed of their attack to counter the most effective element of the Persian army—its archers. As they descended onto the plain, they at first approached the Persians at a steady pace. When they drew within an effective archery range of about 200 yards (183 meters), however, they broke into a brisk trot. This disrupted the aim of the archers while minimizing the time they were exposed to the arrows.

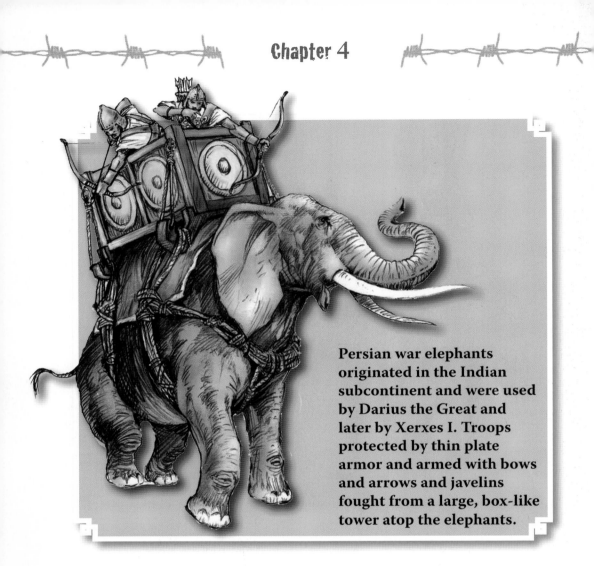

Persian war elephants originated in the Indian subcontinent and were used by Darius the Great and later by Xerxes I. Troops protected by thin plate armor and armed with bows and arrows and javelins fought from a large, box-like tower atop the elephants.

"On came the Greeks, with one unwavering line of levelled spears," wrote military historian Edward Shepherd Creasy, "against which the light targets, the short lances and cimeters [scimitars] of the Orientals, offered weak defence. The front rank of the Asiatics must have gone down to a man at the first shock."[4] But the Persians regrouped quickly and pushed back the weakened Greek line in the center.

The Greeks at the center broke and began to withdraw to the high ground. Their retreat coincided with the success of their attacking comrades on both flanks. As the Persians pursued the fleeing Greeks in the center, the Greeks at either end doubled

The *syntagma* (arrangement) fielded by the Macedonians was developed from the earlier hoplite phalanx. It consisted of 256 foot soldiers called phalangites in a close-ranked rectangular formation. The spears (sarissas) of the first five rows of men projected well beyond the front of the formation and kept enemies at a good distance. Each sarissa was 15 to 18 feet (4.5 to 5.5 meters) long and weighed 12 to 15 pounds (5.5 to 7 kilograms).

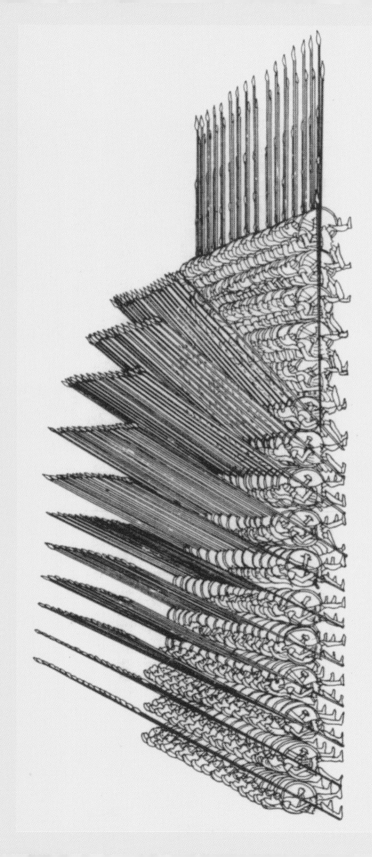

Ancient Greek spears were fitted with an iron spearhead and a bronze butt on a wooden shaft. If a spearhead broke off, the bronze butt could be turned and used as an alternate weapon.

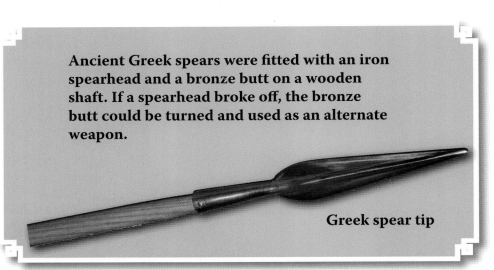

Greek spear tip

Trepaning tool used for boring and bloodletting

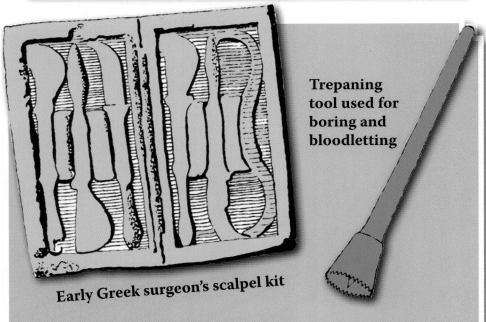

Early Greek surgeon's scalpel kit

Early Greek surgical tools were as crude as the state of the medical practitioner's art in ancient times. More than a few battle survivors later succumbed to infections introduced by the surgeon's knife.

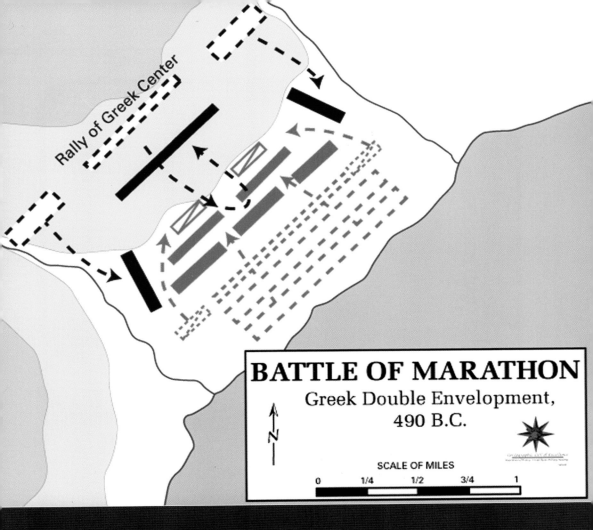

Rally of Greek Center

BATTLE OF MARATHON

Greek Double Envelopment,
490 B.C.

N

SCALE OF MILES

0   1/4   1/2   3/4   1

The double envelopment is a basic military strategy. It results when
an attacking army faces the enemy in front, on both flanks, and in
the rear—in short, when one combatant army surrounds another.

the Persian army back on itself. This maneuver is now known as
a classic double envelopment. When the fleeing Greeks in the
center rallied and returned to the battle, the Persians found
themselves surrounded.

"[O]n the two wings the Athenians and the Plataeans defeated
the enemy," scribed Herodotus. "Having so done, they suffered
the routed barbarians [Persians] to fly at their ease, and joining

Greeks and Persians engaged in mortal combat. Greek hoplites wielded their short swords in hand-to-hand fighting, while Persian archers fired away from a distance.

the two wings in one, fell upon those who had broken their own centre, and fought and conquered them."[5] When the short and bloody fray ended, 6,400 Persians lay dead on the Plain of Marathon. One hundred and ninety-two Greeks died while saving Athens.

Greek Hoplites

During the period of the city-state or *polis* (c.700–300 BCE), Greek military operations relied on heavy infantrymen known as hoplites. Their name derives from cumbersome battle gear called *hopla*. This gear included a corslet (body armor), a helmet, and greaves (shin armor). They were made from bronze about a half inch (1.3 centimeters) thick. Such armor afforded considerable protection from most swords, spears, or missiles (arrows and other penetrating weapons).

The hoplites carried an unusually large wooden shield called a *hoplon.* It weighed some 15 to 20 pounds (7 to 9 kilograms), with a diameter of 3 feet (0.9 meter), and covered half of the infantryman's body.

Each man depended on the man next to him to shield his own unprotected right side and to maintain the phalanx (rank and file) in which they fought. A unique double grip allowed the heavy shield to be held by the left arm alone. Its concave shape enabled the rear ranks to rest it on their shoulders as they pressed ahead. Because of the hoplite's natural tendency to seek protection of his unshielded right side in the shield of his companion to the right, the entire phalanx often drifted to the right on the battlefield.

Offensively, the hoplite depended on a wooden spear 7 to 10 feet (2 to 3 meters) long. He also carried a secondary short iron sword. Massed into columns of the phalanx, hoplites charged their enemies head-on. Under their covering shields, they sought victory through the sheer force of men in each rank pushing against the backs of those in the rank ahead. Hoplite fighting embodied the purest elements of savagery and mayhem.

Athenian phalanx formation

On the Plain of Marathon, the vaunted Persian cavalry distinguished itself only by its absence. Of those Persians who survived the carnage generated by the Greek hoplites, some escaped into the Great Marsh. Others fled to the water's edge, boarded ship, and put to sea, narrowly escaping their pursuers. The Athenians caught up with a few at the shore and set seven galleys aflame. "It was in the struggle here that Callimachus the Polemarch, after greatly distinguishing himself, lost his life,"[1] wrote Herodotus. Plutarch, the famous Greek biographer and author, later reported that the body of Callimachus was pierced by so many spears that it stood upright even in death.

Despite the stunning defeat of the Persians on the plain, Datis and Artaphernes still had hopes of defeating the Greeks and capturing Athens. Instead of sailing for home, the Persian fleet rounded Cape Sunium (now Sounion) and headed for the city. The Persians hoped to reach Athens by sea before the Greeks could return there by land. "But the Athenians with all possible speed marched away to the defence of their city," wrote Herodotus, "and

"The Birth Cry of Europe"

succeeded in reaching Athens before the appearance of the barbarians."[2] After losing the race to Athens, the Persians decided against landing and sailed for home.

Meanwhile, on the morning after the full moon, two thousand spearmen had left Sparta and marched the 150 miles (240 kilometers) to Athens in the remarkable time of three days.[3] "Too late to help, but curious to view the Persian corpses, the Spartans visited the battlefield, where their professional admiration soared for the hitherto unadmired Athenians," noted historian Alan Lloyd. "Indeed, one of the primary consequences of Marathon was the enormous prestige it gave Athens throughout Greece, and the confidence it bestowed on Athenian democracy."[4] The

Athenians buried their 192 fallen warriors in a common grave on the battlefield. Its burial mound forms a major landmark on the Marathon plain, an eternal monument to the improbable—but nonetheless heroic—Athenian victory.

A number of Greeks notable for their future accomplishments fought at Marathon. Among those were the politician Themistocles (theh-MIS-tuh-kleez) and the playwright Aeschylus (ES-kuh-lus). Aeschylus's brother, Cynegirus (sy-NEG-ih-rus), had his hand chopped off by a Persian ax as he laid hold of a ship's stern. Unable to stop his bleeding, he died of his wound. His death spoke of the massive carnage at Marathon.

By most accounts, Miltiades emerged as the foremost hero of Marathon and the singular savior of Athens. The light of his hard-earned glory dimmed quickly, however, in the battle's aftermath. Soon after the Persians had sailed for home, Athenians granted his request for seventy vessels, an armed force, and money for a naval expedition to the Cyclades. In return, he promised them much gold.

"So, Miltiades, having got the armament, sailed against Paros," wrote Herodotus, "with the object, as he alleged, of punishing the Parians for having gone to war with Athens, inasmuch as a trireme of theirs had come with the Persian fleet to Marathon."[5] In reality, Miltiades wanted to settle an old grudge against the Parians for telling a damaging tale about him to a Persian. He landed on Paros and laid siege to its city.

Eventually, after receiving a wound in his thigh and failing to breach the island's defenses, Miltiades returned to Athens. Angry citizens brought him to trial for his life on charges of deceit. Because of his wound, Miltiades appeared in court on a bench and did not testify in his own defense. In consideration of his heroism at Marathon, the people spared his life but fined him fifty talents, a hefty sum in his time. "Soon afterwards," scribed Herodotus, "his thigh completely gangrened and mortified [its tissues died]: and so Miltiades died."[6] His fleeting moment of

After the Battle of Marathon, the Greeks buried their fallen comrades in a mound on the Plain of Marathon. The hallowed mound remains visible to tourists.

fame ended in slow, painful, and inglorious decay. History often treats its heroes harshly.

The fates of Datis and Artaphernes somehow crept off and disappeared in one of the many cracks in time. Darius I, whom many called the Great King, lived on for four more years, still plotting his revenge against Athens and the Greeks. An uprising in Egypt temporarily diverted his attention, and death claimed him while his armies were subduing the revolt. He was interred a few miles north of his winter palace in Persepolis, in a tomb

The Funeral of Miltiades, painted by Jean-Francois-Pierre Peyron in 1782, underscores the heroic status Miltiades achieved at the Battle of Marathon.

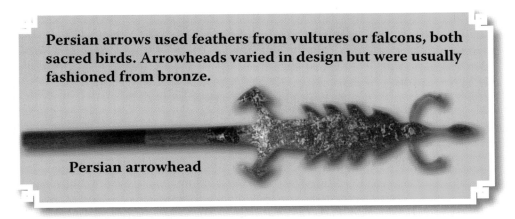

Persian arrows used feathers from vultures or falcons, both sacred birds. Arrowheads varied in design but were usually fashioned from bronze.

Persian arrowhead

hewed from solid rock. His hatred for Athenians passed to his son and successor Xerxes.

Of all the tales of Marathon, few surpass the story of Pheidippides the runner and his triumphant—yet tragic—final run. Bearing the news of the Athenians' great victory to Athens, he raced irrepressibly onward. "Legend tells how he staggered through the city gates, uttered a single exultant cry, and collapsed, dying,"[7] recalled historian Alan Lloyd. That cry, as romanticized by poet Robert Browning, was "Athens is saved!"[8]

The Athenian victory at Marathon was decisive but not conclusive. It did not end the attempts of Persians to extend their empire into Europe. More great battles remained to be fought in what came to be called the Greco-Persian Wars (499–448 BCE). But the Battle of Marathon marked a key turning point. It had set the limits of the Persian Empire. The Greeks—before untested against top military opposition—established themselves on that embattled plain as warriors of the highest caliber. More important, they instilled an unshakable confidence in themselves that would carry them through to future triumphs in defense of freedom and democracy.

Noted military historian J. F. C. Fuller wrote that the Greek victory "endowed the victors with a faith in their destiny which was to endure for three centuries, during which western culture was born. Marathon was the birth cry of Europe."[9]

The Persian Army

Under Cyrus the Great, the Persian army or *kara* consisted of warriors from various Persian tribes. Darius I transformed the *kara* into a professional standing army, or *spada*. The *spada* was made up of the Immortals (imperial bodyguard), cavalry, infantry, and siege troops.

The Persian army was organized on a decimal basis, drawn from earlier Mede and Assyrian formations. A squad consisted of 10 men; a company, 100 men. Ten companies formed a regiment of 1,000 men; and ten regiments formed a division of 10,000 men. Divisions were organized into six field armies. Persian commanders, unlike many of their modern-day counterparts, fought alongside their men and were often killed in action.

Persian nobles began preparing for military service in their youth. Training in companies of 50 men, they were schooled in running, swimming, horse grooming, tilling the land, handicrafts, and standing watch. As they progressed, they learned the art of the chase, both mounted and afoot; archery; tossing the spear and javelin; and how to sustain themselves on forced marches in harsh climates. Nobles entered the military profession at the age of twenty and served until fifty.

The bow was the basic weapon of the Persian army. Both cavalry and infantry used it with deadly efficiency. In battle, Persians avoided close-quarters infantry combat until swarms of their foot archers had totally disorganized their foes from the front. Then their heavier infantry moved in with spear and sword, while their cavalry attacked the flanks.

The Immortals

BCE

559–522 Cyrus II (Cyrus the Great) and his son Cambyses II rule the Persian Empire.

522 Darius I seizes the Persian throne by assassinating the pretender Gaumata.

c.520 Miltiades the Younger establishes himself as tyrant of the Chersonese (Gallipoli Peninsula).

513 Miltiades joins Darius I in an expedition against the Scythians.

512 Darius I of Persia begins to feel threatened by Greece's far-reaching trade routes.

510 Greece represents the only important nation beyond the grasp of the Persian Empire.

510–506 Hippias is dethroned as tyrant of the Athenian city-state.

499–494 Ionian city-states revolt against Persian subjugation.

498 The Ionians burn Sardis.

494 Persian fleet defeats Ionian fleet in naval battle near the island of Lade.

493 Miltiades returns to Athens.

492 Persian army led by Mardonius invades Thrace and Macedonia.

491 Darius I sends envoys to Greek city-states demanding earth and water.

490

July Datis and Artaphernes assemble an invasion force in Cilicia and sail for Athens.

Early August The Persian invasion fleet provokes skirmishes in the Cyclades Campaign.

Late August Datis lands in Euboea and lays siege to Eretria. Callimachus wins honors during the Panathenaic Games in Athens.

Early September Datis and Artaphernes land their invasion force at Schinias Beach.

c.September 21 The Athenians and Eretrians, led by Miltiades and Callimachus, defeat the Persians at the Battle of Marathon. Callimachus is killed in the fighting.

c.September 24 The Spartans arrive.

489 Miltiades dies.

486 Darius I dies.

480 Xerxes I of Persia defeats Thessaly and wins the Battle of Thermopylae. Greek city-states combine to defeat Persian fleet at Salamis.

479 Mardonius is killed at the Battle of Plataea. Greeks destroy the Persian fleet at Mycale.

466 Cimon, Athenian general and son of Miltiades, defeats the Persian fleet and army at Eurymedon River in Asia Minor.

| 450 | Cimon again triumphs over the Persian fleet at Salamis and conquers most of Cyprus. Cimon dies. |
| 448 | The Peace of Callias ends the Greco-Persian Wars. |

History and Technology Timeline

BCE

551	Chinese philosopher K'ung-tzu (Confucius) is born.
c.550	Athens and other Greek city-states become centers of learning and the arts.
539	Cyrus the Great of Persia conquers the Babylonian Empire.
c.520	Persians conquer the Indus Valley.
c.515	Greeks introduce a light crane for lifting heavy loads.
509	Rome expels its king and establishes a republic.
c.500	The northeastern Indian state of Magadha, the "cradle of Buddhism," emerges as a regional power. Etruscan civilization and political power reaches its zenith in Italy. The chariot is introduced in Britain. Greeks develop the trireme as their essential warship. The catapult is invented in Italy.
484	Herodotus, the Greek "Father of History," is born.
480	Persian engineers construct a pontoon bridge to transport Xerxes' invading army across the Hellespont (Dardanelles). Wooden winches are used to tighten support cables. During a siege of Athens, Persian soldiers use arrows wrapped in fiber and soaked in oil—the first known projectile torches.
c.470	Greek philosopher Socrates is born.
c.465	A series of disastrous earthquakes rocks Sparta. People of Syracuse, a seaport city in Sicily, revolt against tyrannical Greek rule and establish a democracy.
458	Citizen-soldier Cincinnatus becomes Roman dictator.
c.450	Iron tool technology spreads across North Africa. Confucianism gains momentum among scholars in China. Rome's first standardized code of laws is placed in the forum in a form known as the Twelve Tables.
445	Athens and Sparta begin 30-year truce; fighting resumes in 415.
443	Pericles is elected general of Athens for fifteen years.
c.440	Judean law forbids marriage between Jews and non-Jews. Pericles presides over the Golden Age of Athens.

Chapter Notes

**Chapter 1. The Vengeance
of Darius**

1. Will Durant, *The Life of Greece* (New York: Simon and Schuster, 1966), p. 234.
2. Herodotus, *The History of Herodotus* (Chicago: Encyclopedia Britannica, 1952), p. 192.
3. Edward Shepherd Creasy, "The Battle of Marathon," in *Fifteen Decisive Battles of the Western World: From Marathon to Waterloo* (New York: Barnes & Noble, 2004), p. 7.
4. Ibid.
5. Alan Lloyd, *Marathon: The Story of Civilizations on Collision Course* (London: Souvenir Press, 2008), p. 115.

Chapter 2. The Ionian Revolt

1. Will Durant, *The Life of Greece* (New York: Simon and Schuster, 1966), p. 235.
2. Ibid.
3. Herodotus, *The History of Herodotus* (Chicago: Encyclopedia Britannica, 1952), p. 181.
4. Ibid.
5. Ibid., p. 182.
6. Ibid.
7. Durant, p. 235.
8. Terrence Poulos, *Extreme War: The Military Book Club's Encyclopedia of the Biggest, Fastest, Bloodiest, and Best in Warfare* (Garden City, NY: Military Book Club, 2004), p. 6.

Chapter 3. Drama at Marathon

1. Herodotus, *The History of Herodotus* (Chicago: Encyclopedia Britannica, 1952), p. 193.
2. Ibid., p. 203.
3. Ibid.
4. Terrence Poulos, *Extreme War: The Military Book Club's Encyclopedia of the Biggest, Fastest, Bloodiest, and Best in Warfare* (Garden City, NY: Military Book Club, 2004), p. 17.
5. Herodotus, p. 205.
6. Ibid.

Chapter 4. Saving Athens

1. Terrence Poulos, *Extreme War: The Military Book Club's Encyclopedia of the Biggest, Fastest, Bloodiest, and Best in Warfare* (Garden City, NY: Military Book Club, 2004), p. 17.
2. Herodotus, *The History of Herodotus* (Chicago: Encyclopedia Britannica, 1952), p. 207.
3. Ibid.
4. Edward Shepherd Creasy, "The Battle of Marathon," in *Fifteen Decisive Battles of the Western World: From Marathon to Waterloo* (New York: Barnes & Noble, 2004), p. 22.
5. Herodotus, p. 207.

Chapter Notes

Chapter 5. "The Birth Cry of Europe"

1. Herodotus, *The History of Herodotus* (Chicago: Encyclopedia Britannica, 1952), p. 207.
2. Ibid., p. 208.
3. Alan Lloyd, *Marathon: The Story of Civilizations on Collision Course* (London: Souvenir Press, 2008), pp. 204–205.
4. Herodotus, p. 211.
5. Ibid., p. 212.
6. Lloyd, p. 208.
7. Ibid.
8. Paul K. Davis, *100 Decisive Battles: From Ancient Times to the Present* (New York: Oxford University Press, 1999), p. 13.
9. Will Durant, *The Life of Greece* (New York: Simon and Schuster, 1966), p. 242.

Further Reading

Books

Califf, David J. *Marathon. Battles That Changed the World.* New York: Chelsea House Publishers, 2002.

Crompton, Samuel Willard. *Cyrus the Great.* New York: Chelsea House Publishers, 2008.

Roberts, Russell. *How'd They Do That in Ancient Greece?* Hockessin, DE: Mitchell Lane Publishers, 2010.

Ross, Stewart. *Athens Is Saved: The First Marathon.* London, UK: Cherrytree Books, 2007.

Souza, Philip de. *The Greek and Persian Wars 499–386 BC.* Essential History. New York: Routledge, 2003.

Whiting, Jim. *Herodotus.* Hockessin, DE: Mitchell Lane Publishers, 2006.

Works Consulted

Archer, Christon I., John R. Ferris, Holger H. Herwig, and Timothy H. E. Travers. *World History of Warfare*. Lincoln: University of Nebraska Press, 2002.

Cowley, Robert, and Geoffrey Parker (editors). *The Reader's Companion to Military History*. Boston: Houghton Mifflin Company, 1996.

Creasy, Edward Shepherd. *Fifteen Decisive Battles of the Western World: From Marathon to Waterloo*. New York: Barnes & Noble, 2004.

Davis, Paul K. *100 Decisive Battles: From Ancient Times to the Present*. New York: Oxford University Press, 1999.

Dupuy, R. Ernest, and Trevor N. Dupuy. *The Encyclopedia of Military History*. Rev. ed. New York: Harper & Row, 1977.

Dupuy, Trevor N., Curt John, and David L. Bongard. *The Harper Encyclopedia of Military Biography*. New York: HarperCollins, 1992.

Durant, Will. *The Life of Greece*. The Story of Civilization, Vol. 2. New York: Simon and Schuster, 1966.

Eggenberger, David. *An Encyclopedia of Battles: Accounts of Over 1,560 Battles from 1479 B.C. to the Present*. New York: Dover Publications, 1985.

Gilbert, Asrian. *The Encyclopedia of Warfare: From Earliest Times to the Present Day*. Guilford, CT: Lyons Press, 2002.

Hanson, Victor Davis. *Ripples of Battle: How Wars of the Past Still Determine How We Fight, How We Live, and How We Think*. New York: Doubleday, 2003.

Herodotus. *The History of Herodotus*. Robert Maynard Hutchens, Editor in Chief. Chicago: Encyclopedia Britannica, 1952.

Hogg, Ian V. *The Hutchinson Dictionary of Battles*. Oxford, UK: Helicon Publishing, 1998.

Kagan, Neil. *National Geographic Concise History of the World*. Washington, DC: National Geographic, 2006.

Lloyd, Alan. *Marathon: The Story of Civilizations on Collision Course*. London: Souvenir Press, 2008.

Margiotta, Franklin D. (editor). *Brassey's Encyclopedia of Land Forces and Warfare*. Washington, DC: Brassey's, 1996.

———. *Brassey's Encyclopedia of Military History and Biography*. Washington, DC: Brassey's, 1994.

Parker, Geoffrey (editor). *The Cambridge Illustrated History of Warfare: The Triumph of the West*. New York: Cambridge University Press, 1995.

Perrett, Bryan. *The Battle Book: Crucial Conflicts in History from 1469 BC to the Present*. London: Arms and Armour, 1992.

Poulos, Terrence. *Extreme War: The Military Book Club's Encyclopedia of the Biggest, Fastest, Bloodiest, and Best in Warfare*. Garden City, NY: Military Book Club, 2004.

Pratt, Fletcher. *The Battles That Changed History*. Minneola, NY: Dover Publications, 2000.

Sekunda, Nicholas. *Marathon 490 BC: The First Persian Invasion of Greece*. New York: Osprey Publishing, 2002.

Stephenson, Michael (editor). *Battlegrounds: Geography and the History of Warfare*. Washington, DC: National Geographic Society, 2003.

On the Internet

Ancient Mesopotamia: Battle of Marathon
http://joseph_berrigan.tripod.com/ancientbabylon/id27.html
EyeWitness to History: The Battle of Marathon, 490 BC
http://eyewitnesstohistory.com/pfmarathon.htm
History for Kids: The Persians
http://www.historyforkids.org/learn/westasia/history/persians.htm

The approximate present-day location of the Marathon battle line

archon (AR-kon)—One of three Athenian officials who presided over the government.

Chersonese (KUR-suh-neez)—Literally "peninsula"; applied herein to what is now the Gallipoli Peninsula in Turkey.

city-state (SIH-tee-stayt)—A self-governing region in ancient Greece that included a city and the surrounding territory.

envoy (EN-voy, or ON-voy)—A messenger or representative delegated to represent one nation to another.

hoplite (HOP-lyt)—A heavily armed and armored infantryman of ancient Greece.

Panathenaic (pan-ath-uh-NAY-ik) **Games**—Sporting events that were held every four years in Athens. Hosted in a stadium, they incorporated religious festivals, athletic competitions, and cultural events.

phalanx (FAY-lanks)—A standard military formation used by the ancient Greeks; it consisted of ranks of spearmen in a unit that was usually eight ranks deep.

polemarch (POH-luh-march)—A commander in war and judge in court cases involving foreigners.

polis (POH-lis)—A city-state.

satrap (SAY-trap)—A governor of a province in ancient Persia.

strategoi (STRAT-uh-goy)—Ten generals who commanded the military units of the ten Athenian tribes.

subjugation (sub-juh-GAY-shun)—The act of becoming a subject (one who is ruled by another).

trireme (TRY-reem)—An ancient galley (ship) with three banks of oars.

Twelve Ionian Cities—An Ionian religious league made up of ten mainland city-states and two island city-states: Miletus, Myus, Priene, Samos, Ephesus, Colophon, Lebedos, Teos, Erythrae, Chios, Clazomenae, and Phocaea.

tyrant (TY-runt)—In ancient times, anyone who established his rule by force.

Index